Ge
Washington

SADDLEBACK
EDUCATIONAL PUBLISHING

Saddleback's Graphic Biographies

SADDLEBACK
EDUCATIONAL PUBLISHING
www.sdlback.com

Copyright © 2008 by Saddleback Educational Publishing
All rights reserved. No part of this book may be reproduced in any form or by any means, electronic or mechanical, including photocopying, recording, or by any information storage and retrieval system without the written permission of the publisher. SADDLEBACK EDUCATIONAL PUBLISHING and any associated logos are trademarks and/or registered trademarks of Saddleback Educational Publishing.

ISBN-10: 1-59905-223-7
ISBN-13: 978-1-59905-223-6
eBook: 978-1-60291-586-2

Printed in Malaysia

20 19 18 17 16   2 3 4 5 6

When George Washington was born in 1732, there was no United States. The American colonies belonged to England. He led the army that fought for and won our freedom. He helped to form our government. He became our first president.

But that was the man of the future. As a farm boy in Virginia, he loved to ride horses and to tame unbroken colts.

He loved outdoor things— hunting, fishing, swimming, boating. He did not like school as much, but he worked at his lessons.

Read your exercise, George.

Yes, sir. Surveying the art of measuring land ...

Your spelling is very bad. But you are ahead of the class in arithmetic.

I like figuring.

When he was eleven, his father died. His half-brother, Lawrence, became like a father to him.

I am afraid there isn't enough money now to send you to England to school.

I can study alone. And I learn from listening to you and your friends.

Later, he found out how to combine his gift for figuring and his love for the outdoors.

Could I learn to be a surveyor?

That would be good work for you! Thousands of miles of country need to be measured and mapped.

At fifteen he became a surveyor's helper to learn the job.

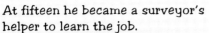

I'll have this map finished in an hour.

Good.

His hard work paid off with a great opportunity.

Lord Fairfax is sending a party over the mountains to survey his great tract of land. You may go if you wish.

If I wish? It's too good to be true!

He was well paid, but he would have gone for nothing for the chance to explore the wilderness—to learn to live in it—and to meet the pioneer settlers.

Howdy, folks. Come in.

How did one man, without slaves or servants, clear this land and build the cabin?

They shot game for food.

They camped in the wilderness.

George, you're becoming a good cook!

George had seen few Native Americans before. One night they watched a war dance.

The music comes from a pot half full of water with a deerskin stretched over it ... George wrote in his diary.

When he was seventeen, he passed a test and became a licensed surveyor. But he did not spend all of his time working.

He learned to dance and enjoyed it all of his life.

You dance well, sir.

He loved the fox hunts that were popular. No one could outride him.

In 1752 he was saddened by the death of Lawrence. He inherited responsibilities, including the estate of Mount Vernon.

He also became Major George Washington of the Virginia militia.

Congratulations, Major.

I only hope, sir, that I can do half as fine a job as Lawrence did in training our troops.

England and France were rivals for American land. On surveying trips, George heard talk from traders and trappers.

The French are building forts all the way from Canada to Ohio. They mean to take our land.

They're stirring up the Native Americans to fight us. They won't let us trap in the Ohio country.

But the Ohio country is claimed by Virginia! I'll see Governor Dinwiddie.

He talked with the Virginia governor.

I have been told by King George to send a letter demanding that the French withdraw.

I want to deliver that message.

I accept! It will be a hard winter trip through the mountains.

Your message shall be delivered to the French commander, sir!

For forty-one days George and his party traveled on rough paths, through rain and snow, across dangerous waters.

Watch the luggage! Don't let it tip.

The French commander welcomed George politely, but his answer was firm.

France claims this land! We will build more forts. We will drive out any English who come here.

George talked with the scout who was his guide.

I must hurry back with the French answer; and with information about the French and the Native Americans.

The horses are thinner and weaker every day.

Then we will leave them and the rest of the party to follow slowly. You and I will go on foot!

They plodded many miles through heavy snow.

They escaped an Indian ambush.

Rafting across a great, ice-choked river, George fell in and swam for his life.

Look out!

But they arrived safely. Governor Dinwiddie was pleased with the hard, fast trip George had made. He formed new plans.

Major, I want you to lead a force of men against the French. Build a fort at the fork of the Ohio River.

I will do my best, sir.

The men George led were too few to fight the French army. Badly defeated, they surrendered their arms and marched back to Virginia.

But people began to know that George Washington was brave and strong and a good leader.

The English king sent an army to Virginia to fight the French.

General Braddock and the British regulars.

Aren't they grand in their red coats?

They'll send the French flying.

But *George* did not think so. He was appointed to guide Braddock.

Sir, in the wilderness, the men's red coats and solid marching columns will make them an easy target for the Native Americans.

The savages may be dangerous to your raw American troops—but upon the King's regulars, they won't make any impression!

Alas, *George* was right. Near the French fort, the French and Native Americans attacked Braddock's army and cut it to pieces.

George fought fiercely. Bullets went through his hat and clothes. Two horses were shot from under him.

Take cover! Shoot when you can see your enemy.

Most of the Virginians escaped safely. George had taught them his knowledge of fighting.

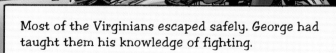

The war between France and England lasted for seven years. George fought many times and became a well-known leader. The French were driven back to Canada.

And there were happier events. On January 6, 1759, he married Martha Custis, a pretty, young widow.

He took her and her two children, Jack and Patsy, home to Mt. Vernon.

I have been away too long. It is much neglected.

Together we will make it a happy home and a fine plantation!

He enjoyed his family.

I do not know one note from another, but I enjoy hearing Patsy play.

He learned to be a good farmer.

We must try other crops. Too much tobacco-growing ruins the soil.

The year of his marriage he was elected to the Virginia House of Burgesses.*

February 22, your birthday and the day you first attend the House.

My part will be small at first. But I will learn about lawmaking and what laws are good and bad.

For fifteen years, George was happy at Mt. Vernon. He became an important man in Virginia.

Then trouble came to the colonies.

The new English laws take away our rights and our liberties, and they grow worse all the time.

What can be done?

We must unite and stand up for our freedom! Delegates from each colony will meet in Philadelphia to discuss it.

The colonists grew angrier. It looked as if they would be forced to fight. George was a delegate to the first Continental Congress. In April 1775 he prepared to leave for the second one.

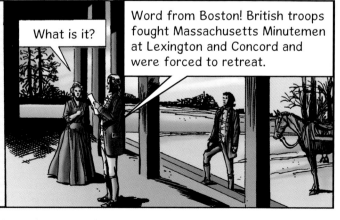

What is it?

Word from Boston! British troops fought Massachusetts Minutemen at Lexington and Concord and were forced to retreat.

* The popular branch of the legislature of colonial Maryland and Virginia

The American Revolution had begun! Delegates hurried to Philadelphia, Washington among them.

The British hold Boston and its port. Men from the New England colonies surround Boston. We must send soldiers to help them!

We need an army ... a united colonial army!

And we need a general for that army!

On June 14, John Adams of Massachusetts rose to speak to the Congress.

I have but one man in mind as commander in chief, a gentleman from Virginia, George Washington!

Hear! Hear!

He was unanimously elected by the Congress. One of his first official acts was to review several nearby militia companies.

He knew he had accepted an almost impossible task. He wrote to Martha.

My Dearest ... I should enjoy more happiness in one month with you at home than in fifty years abroad ... but the American cause has been under my care. I hope to return to you in the fall.

Neither of them could know that it would be eight years before he would see Mt. Vernon again.

He went to Boston to take charge of the army that was trying to drive out the British.

They are farmers, shopkeepers, trappers, scouts, few are soldiers.

They are brave Americans. It is my job to teach them to fight.

It was also his job to get them food and guns.

There are 8,200 men on the rolls, 5,600 present and fit for duty. Two thousand are without guns.

Henry Knox was one of his colonels.

Can you go to Fort Ticonderoga and bring back the British cannons captured there?

I'll do my best, sir.

And several months later, the men surrounding Boston cheered a welcome sight.

It's Colonel Knox and his men!

They dragged sixty-six pieces of artillery through the snow all the way from New York State.

Washington inspired such love in his men that they would often do what seemed impossible. This was a great gift.

Spring came. The men were better trained. A supply of ammunition had been built up.

In darkness, without a sound, our men must drag the cannons to the heights over Boston and take the British by surprise.

At daybreak, the British found themselves in a trap, bombarded by American cannons. They gave up and sailed away. The Americans marched into Boston.

Hurray for General Washington!

And hurray for the new American flag!

But Washington knew the war was only the beginning.

I will take most of the army to New York. I think the English will strike there next.

In New York, he received information.

The British are sending German troops—Hessians—to fight in America!

They will hire Hessian troops to fight their fellow Englishmen? Disgraceful!

There was other news.

Sir, news from Philadelphia. Independence!

We are now the United States of America!

The Declaration of Independence had been signed. It was read to all the troops. Celebrating patriots pulled down a statue of King George.

Melt him into bullets to shoot his soldiers!

But the British landed 20,000 troops. The life of the new nation hung by a thread. The Americans fought, lost, and retreated.

We must slip away, again and again, until we have built an army strong enough to beat the British. There is still hope if they cannot destroy us.

By Christmas, the British had pushed them through New Jersey and across the Delaware River.

The Hessians at Trenton across the river will be celebrating Christmas. It is snowing. The river is full of ice.

The Hessians will never expect an attack. We will surprise them.

In the bitter weather, the Americans crossed the river in small boats.

The surprise was complete. The Hessians tumbled from their beds only to surrender. Trenton was captured along with 1,000 Hessian soldiers.

A victory was wonderful. But the year that followed was bad, with many defeats. In January, Washington's army went into winter camp at Valley Forge.

I will move into it only when all my men are housed.

There was timber for building but very little else.

Then, foreign volunteers arrived to support the American fight for freedom. Among them was the young Marquis de Lafayette from France.

My staff is called my family. I shall hereafter, dear sir, regard you as a member of it.

I shall be happy and honored.

This was the start of a close life-long friendship.

Martha came to turn headquarters into a home.

I have come to cheer up my old soldier.

Just the sight of you does that, my dear.

And at last supplies began to come in.

Meat and grain from the quartermaster, sir.

And I have word a supply of clothing is on the way!

Baron von Steuben came from Prussia and drilled the troops. They laughed at his broken English and worked hard for him.

He is making my country boys into soldiers at last!

April came ... warmer weather ... and great news. France had joined the United States! She would send money, ships, supplies!

Valley Forge celebrated.

Long live the King of France!

Long live the United States of America!

But there were other bad times and three more years of war still ahead.

The British have moved south. They've taken Georgia. Charleston has fallen with 5,500 troops captured!

What one thing would help the most?

A navy! To pin down the British troops.

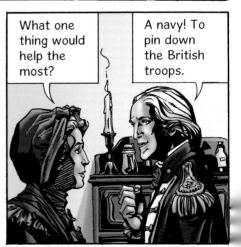

In Connecticut in 1781, Washington met with the French General Rochambeau.

General, two French fleets are sailing toward America! Where shall they fight?

Wonderful news! We will trick the British into thinking we plan to attack New York.

Instead we will march south quickly. We will attack Cornwallis and Yorktown from land while the French fleet prevents his rescue by sea.

The plan worked perfectly. While the French ships bottled up Yorktown harbor, the American and French armies moved in from land to bombard the town.

On October 17, a white flag appeared. Cornwallis surrendered. While Washington watched, and the stars and stripes waved, the British army marched out to lay down its arms.

There were more battles, but after Yorktown the American cause was safe. In 1783 a peace treaty was signed. At last, Washington said goodbye to his officers.

With a heart full of love and gratitude I take leave of you.

In a few days he reached home.

You'll soon be fox hunting again, General.

The next morning, the aides who rode home with him were surprised. They had never seen him out of uniform.

Gentlemen, this is how I shall be from now on—a man of private life!

But the new country faced many problems.

The country is divided. Each state thinks of its own needs. The central government has no power to enforce the laws or raise money.

In 1787 he went as a delegate to the new Philadelphia convention. He was elected chairman.

I hope you will forgive my errors. They will be unintentional.

Through a long, hot summer the delegates argued. At last a document was put together. When accepted by the states, it became our constitution.

There was one thing everyone agreed on. The *New York Journal* on April 2, 1788, carried the following notice.

... It appears that illustrious soldier and venerated citizen, George Washington Esquire is unanimously elected President of the United States.

From this country and Europe, letters poured in urging him to serve.

Alexander Hamilton says the survival of the new government might depend on my acceptance. I fear it is my duty. Once things are running smoothly perhaps I can resign.

Once again, the day came when he had to leave his beloved Mt. Vernon.

How do you feel, my dear?

Somewhat like a prisoner going to his execution. This is the end of domestic peace. But thank heaven you will soon join me in exile.

As always when he traveled, people in every village and town turned out to show their love and respect.

In New York City, on April 30, 1789, Washington took the oath of office as the first President of the United States of America.

He made Alexander Hamilton his secretary of the treasury.

We must raise money to run the government and pay our debts.

I will draw up a plan, sir. I hope it will work.

Thomas Jefferson became his secretary of state.

Hamilton and I in the same cabinet are like two roosters in a pit. We argue about almost every issue.

You both have the good of the country at heart.

He served two four-year terms. The president and the country faced many problems. But with his gift for persuading men to work together, even when their views differed ... and with the love and respect the people felt for Washington himself ... he made this new form of government begin to work.

Among his more pleasant jobs was the planning of a new capital city to be built on the Potomac River.

It was later named Washington in his honor.

At last, in 1797 he retired to the home he loved.

How does it feel to be home?

Like a school boy on holiday!

For two years, he enjoyed his family. In 1799 after a day spent riding through his fields in sleet and snow, he became ill. Two days later he died. All over the world, people mourned.

Henry Lee, governor of Virginia and one of Washington's old soldiers, spoke at a memorial service.

First in war, first in peace, and first in the hearts of his countrymen.

At his own wish, he was buried in a simple tomb at Mt. Vernon. Later, Martha was buried beside him.

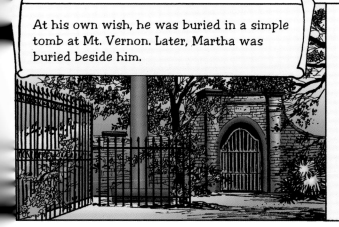

Here millions of Americans have come through the years to honor the memory of George Washington, truly the father of this country.

THE END